INDIAN (HINDU) WEDDING CEREMONIES

A STEP BY STEP GUIDE

KAMAL AGARWAL

ISBN 979-8-89322-768-0

Dedicated To

My Mother (Chhaya)

My Wife (Meenakshi)

(Both left us early in the prime of their life)

and

My Family who continues to support and inspire me

Disclaimer

This compilation is from my own experiences.

The said narrative is not binding on anybody and there is no intent to harm anybody or any feelings or sentiments whatsoever.

If any occurrence coincides with some other, it is purely accidental and not intentional.

This narrative is to be treated solely as a guideline.

Contents

Foreword

A wedding/marriage in the family is a very important and life-altering occasion, not only for the to-be newlyweds but also both the families as it is also the union of these families for life.

Weddings/Marriages are an important rite of passage in any individual's life from any religion or culture. It is the union of 2 families through the joining of their children in marriage. It marks one's true entry into adulthood, marking him or her fit for taking on the responsibility of the well-being of another human being.

In historical times, Kings used to get married multiple times for various reasons:

- To strengthen their kingdoms by forging alliances with other kingdoms through marriage.

- To produce an heir (male).

In the current scenario, with the fast pace of life, joint families are becoming a thing of the past and are getting replaced by nuclear families. So, when we need to get our children married, we feel a strange helplessness and inadequacy regarding what/when & how to do?

In 2016, when I finalised the marriage of my daughter, I faced a feeling of helplessness as how to go about the whole thing. In the blink of an eye, close to 28 years had passed since my own marriage, and as my mother was no longer with us, who do I turn to now for guidance? It was only after a tedious process of enquiring from elders/family/friends and the boy's family that I was able to put together a fair picture of the various stages of marriage and went on to carry out my daughter's marriage successfully.

I had then noted down the various steps of marriage for my own reference (also to refresh my own memory as my son was still to get married).

Thanks to my notes,I had no problems during the marriage of my son (in 2021) – I actually shared this with my Samdhi who was also going through a similar phase, as I did in 2016 during my daughter's marriage.I've also shared my experiences with friends who have found my notes very helpful while solemnising their children's marriages.

As I had faced a problem, I thought of detailing/writing an account of the various stages of marriage more elaborately so that others could benefit from it.

In a marriage, all the ceremonies/rituals are precursors to the main one, which is Saptapadi (Seven Steps), where the bride and groom take 7 rounds around Agni (Fire) and utter the 7 vows of marriage.

Note: This booklet/guide is only meant as a guideline and is not binding on anyone.

Functions/Rituals of A Typical Indian (Hindu) Marriage

1. Invitation Cards

2. Roka

3. Pre-wedding shoot

4. Mehndi/Ladies Sangeet/Cocktails

5. Engagement/Tilak/GodhBharai/Cocktails

6. Haldi/Bhaat

7. Marriage

    Baarat Gathering Point

    Reception of baarat

    Korath

    Chattri

    Jaimaal

Sajan Goth

Phere

Bidaai

– Throwing of wheat/rice over her head by the newlywed bride

8. After returning home

Haldi ke Hand Impression

Channd

Find the Ring

9. Mukh Dikhaye

10. Pat Phere

11. Honeymoon

The above are the functions that are normally carried out/ held for a typical Indian (Hindu) Marriage. **Depending on the individual's desires, these functions can be interspersed with cocktails or be lavish, moderate, or simple affairs.**

The Functions/Rituals are explained in detail in the next pages as carried out by me.

1. ROKA

Roka

This marks the beginning of the marriage, meaning that the boy and the girl are in agreement for spending their lives together, and both the families are in agreement and have given their blessings for the proposed nuptials.

This ceremony signifies that the match is finalised, and the boy is mine (girl's side), and the girl is ours (boy's side). Nowadays, the Roka ceremony has become a norm for marriage across the board (generally, all communities are now following this).

For instance, when I got married (1989), the Roka ceremony was not being carried out in the Baniya community as it was not considered necessary, and one would go straight to the Engagement and other ceremonies. However, due to the widespread use of computers, the internet, nowadays WhatsApp, Roka has begun to be deemed as an integral ceremony of weddings.

During this ceremony, the girl's brother/s do tika (apply tilak) and give token gifts like guineas/shagun envelopes, etc., to the boy, his parents, and close relatives or friends (attending). The shagun is as per individual person's desires.

Similarly, the boy's parents do tika (apply tilak) and give the girl a ring/necklace/set/shagun envelope (as per desire). Generally, the girl's parents/relatives/friends are not given anything.

Fruit baskets/dry fruits/sweets are exchanged between both the boy's and girl's families to be distributed among relatives and friends.

The Roka ceremony is generally done within the family so that if there is a falling out or the alliance is broken it does not entail getting a bad name, 'badnami.' However, nowadays, the annulment of Roka is not taken to be a slur, as was the case a few years back. However, a long gap between the Roka and marriage is not recommended as it may lead to the disruption of relations.

The scale of this ceremony is dependent on the individual's desires.

2. PRE-WEDDING SHOOT

Pre-Wedding Shoot

Nowadays, the couple-to-be wants to get some together photos taken by the photographer (contracted to take photos of the marriage). Normally, the same photographer covers both families' events.

This is carried out at a farmhouse or resort or any other location mutually decided upon.

3. INVITATION CARDS

Invitation Cards

After the Roka has been completed, Panditji is consulted to take out auspicious dates (as per the Panchang – Hindi calendar) for performing the marriage. After this, both families get together and decide on a date (from within dates given by the Panditji) for the marriage function, which is suitable for both sides.

Once the marriage day and date are finalised, the date of the Engagement/Tilak/GodhBharai is also finalised – this date is generally only 1 or 2 days before the marriage as nowadays relatives/friends coming from out of station do not prefer to stay for long durations due to pressures of work/other commitments.

Earlier, cards were distributed along with some sweets/dry fruits to the local invitees by hand. Nowadays, especially after COVID, the practice of sending E-cards has become prevalent, and physical cards are given only to extremely close relations like Samdhi's, amongst others.

The cards to be sent are:

- Save the date cards so that the invitees can keep that day/s free for attending the marriage ceremonies.

- Engagement – Tilak/GodhBharai.

- Marriage.

(The Engagement and Marriage Cards should also have cards/tokens for the Driver's dinners)

4. MEHNDI (HENNA) + LADIES SANGEET + COCKTAILS

Mehndi (Henna) + Ladies Sangeet + Cocktails

Nowadays, the above 3 are generally combined into one function. Earlier, these used to be done separately.

Mehndi – Ladies attending can get mehndi put simply or elaborately as desired.

Ladies Sangeet – Ladies sing and music is played to add gaiety in the air.

Girls Mehndi

Is done by different artists separately as it takes around 3 – 4 hours as it's very elaborate and covers the arms till the elbows and feet almost till the knees.

Flower Jewellery: sometimes, the girl wears flower jewellery while getting mehndi put.

Boys Mehndi

The boy is also supposed to get mehndi applied (it's considered auspicious). However, the boys, in most cases, get a small dot of henna on the palm to complete the formality of henna.

5. ENGAGEMENT

Engagement

In this ceremony, the boy and girl formally exchange rings, marking the completion of the 1st phase of the marriage process. Nowadays, the (ring exchange is done), the Engagement is coupled with the tilak + godh bharai functions.

Sweets/fruits/dry fruits are exchanged as decided upon.

Tilak

This is a ceremony in which the girl's brother(s) give the (groom) boy gifts such as a watch/perfume/clothes/chain, and other items which are considered necessary for a person's daily needs.

Normally, the suit/kurta set worn by the boy is from the girl's side.

From the boy's side, the girl's brother/s is/are presented with shagun/clothes, etc.

Milni– as the word implies, to meet the boy's relatives and friends.

During/after the tilak ceremony is over, the girl's parents go around with the boy's parents and meet the boy's side relatives and friends and give **Milni** (shagun envelopes could be cash or silver coins, etc, as decided upon).

GodhBharai

In this ceremony, the boy's mother gives the girl (bride) clothes/ jewellery/toiletries, etc. The girl wears a lehenga/saree given by the boy's side.

Cocktails and Dinner

The guests partake in the cocktails and dinner, which are served concurrently with the above functions.

Generally, there is dancing and music during the Engagement ceremony when the families to be united, entertain the guests. General revelry.

The guests are given back presents like chocolate hampers/ silver gifts etc.

The following events are specific to each family and done separately. Normally, these are sandwiched in between the Tilak and Marriage days.

6. HALDI & BHAAT

Haldi

Haldi – the boy/girl is made to sit on a stool/lawn, and Pandit Ji does puja. After which 5 (minimum) people (mother, mausi, sister, brother, etc.) dip the grass handle (made from doob a type of grass) in curd/roli/haldi and apply it to the boy/girl's feet/knees/hands/shoulder/head. After this, the cycle is reversed head/shoulder/hands/knees/feet.

Sometimes, this can get a little out of hand as brothers and sisters, and friends generally tend to treat this as Holi by applying haldi in all possible places of the boy/girl – it turns into a free-for-all. Good fun. Boy's haldi is done at their place, and girl's at her place.

Bhaat

A function where the (maternal uncle) mama/s applies tilak to the parents and near relatives and gives shagun (cash or silver ornaments or jewellery). This is carried out separately at the boy's and girl's places.

7. MARRIAGE

Marriage

Before the baraat leaves for the marriage venue, it is customary to pay obeisance at the temple to seek God's blessings.

1. *Baraat gathering point* – All the guests invited from the boy's side do not arrive with the marriage procession from home – some join at the baraat gathering point while others may reach the venue directly. At the gathering point of the baraat, arrangements of soft drinks/tea/snacks/dry fruits are made to welcome the baratis to the girl's home (the marriage venue).

    From here, the baraat departs for the marriage venue amid a band playing and dancing by the baaratis.

2. *Reception* of *baraat* – the girl's brother helps the boy off the horse / or from the car (the boy steps on a small wooden stool or patra) and brings him inside the marriage venue where the girl's mother is waiting with aarti (welcome).

The other baaratis are welcomed with small garlands for the men and rose buds for the ladies. Perfume (Sugandh) is sprayed over the heads of the guests.

3. *Korath* – In this ritual, the girl's father officially invites the boy's side for the marriage function, and wedding cards of both sides are exchanged along with a Lagan Patrika (made by Panditji) and gifts of silver, etc.

   Lagan Patrika – this contains the names of the boy and girl and their family members who are witnesses to the marriage, along with the dates as per both the Hindu calendar and the English one. This is the official document of marriage registration as per Hindu religion.

4. *Chattri* – The girl is brought from her chamber/room under a chattri (canopy) of flowers which is held by the brothers/friends.

5. *Jaimal* – a ceremony when the girl and boy exchange garlands as a preamble to proceedings in the lagan mandap.

   Then the boy and girl garland each other and then sit on the stage/dais where the visiting guests can meet them and give the customary shagun (envelopes with money/gifts etc).

6. *Sajan goth* – After most of the guests (both from the boy and girl's side) have eaten, a separate table is laid for the boy and girl and the boy's parents, close relatives/friends to partake in food, which is served by the girl's family. After this, people proceed to the lagan Mandap for the pheras.

7. *Pheras* (rounds around the fire (Agni)) – The final step in solemnising the marriage. The boy and girl are seated on chairs/stools. Pundits from both sides start performing the marriage rituals leading to the pheras – 7 in total, of which 5 are main and the girl leads in these and the boy in balance 2 (at least 4 pheras are to be done – these signify the 4 main aims of life, i.e., dharma, arth, kaamand moksha).

The boy's sister ties the knot between the boy's dupatta and girl's saree, signifying their union together.

Kanyadaan – (literal meaning giving (daan) the girl (kanya) away)

The girl's father does kanyadan (application of haldi on girl's palms/legs/right thumb) and the boy applies roli on the girl's maang (Partition between hair) with his Engagement ring.

While pheras are underway the girl's sister/s/friends hide the boy's shoes which are returned after they are given money by the boy.

Lo behold, the marriage is solemnised as per Indian standards.

Significance of taking pheras around Agni (fire):

Of the 5 elements (Prithvi, Akash, Jal, Vayu, and Agni), Agni is the only element, which is pure and cannot get polluted, therefore, in any Hindu Marriage ceremony, couples take their vow with Agni as a witness. For example, in Ramayana, Lord Rama asks Sita to pass

through fire (Agni) to prove her chastity after being released from Ravana's captivity.

8. *Bidaai* – After the completion of pheras, it is time for bidding farewell to the newly married couple and baratis. Normally shawls or some small silver ornament is given to the boy's father and close male family members.

The girl's parents, bua, mausi, and mami, apply tilak to the girl and boy and give gifts (jewellery, cash) and bid them well.

When the girl is leaving her house (marriage venue) she throws handfuls of wheat/rice over her head and behind. The significance is that her parent's house should continue to flourish even though she has gone to her new home this also signifies that she is repaying her parents for her upbringing etc.

The car in which the newlywed couple depart for home is decorated with flowers and is driven by the groom's brother-in-law (he is given shagun for performing this task).

8. AFTER RETURNING HOME

9. MUKH DIKHAYI

10. PAT PHERE

11. HONEYMOON

After Reaching Home

The boy's mother welcomes the newlyweds with aarti and applies tilak (tika) on their foreheads.

Haldi ke hand Impression: The bride is made to imprint her palm impressions on the wall at the entry of the house. This could also be done on paper instead of the wall or window. The impression is of turmeric (considered to be auspicious).

The bride is also made to overturn a utensil(kalash) full of rice (the significance is she is bringing prosperity to the house).

A girl is considered to be the Lakshmi (good luck). For instance, when a girl is born in any household, we say Lakshmi aa gayi – good fortune has come. Thus, we have the ritual of the girl throwing rice back in her parent's house upon being bid farewell (Bidaai) from her parent's house and knocking over the utensil of rice in her new home.

So that both households can continue to prosper.

Now the newlyweds are made to play 2 games:

1. Saying Channds (Riddles) – this is now seldom done.

2. Find the Ring -In a utensil full of water/milk covered with rose petals, a ring is hidden. The newlyweds have to dip their hands in the utensil and find the ring. The person finding the ring 1st is supposed to be the dominant partner in the marriage.

Finally, the newlyweds get to go to their room (which is decorated with flowers). They are now alone together alone to consummate their union.

In the morning, the last 2 rituals are to be completed.

Mukh Dhikhayi

In the morning after the marriage, it's time for the guest's (relatives and friends who are staying there or coming by in the morning) departure. They apply tilak to the newlyweds and give shagun (envelopes with money/gifts/jewellery etc.) and see the bride's face.

Pat Phere

The girl's brother comes to pick up his sister and takes her to her maternal home from where the boy comes to pick up his wife and takes her away.

The couple is given gifts by the girl's parents upon their departure.

Honeymoon

All the marriage ceremonies, etc, have now been completed, and it's time for the newlyweds to depart for their honeymoon. People go abroad to exotic destinations or within the Country as per choice.

The purpose of going on honeymoon is for the newlyweds to get to know each other emotionally as well as physically. It's also a vacation from the hectic days of marriage functions.

Marriage Vows

The Seven Sacred Vows of marriage are described as follows broadly:

- The bride and groom promise to love each other solely and promise to fulfil their respective roles in their lives.

- The boy promises - Together, we will protect our house and children. The girl, in return, promises, "I will be by your side as your courage and strength."

- The boy and girl promise - May we grow wealthy and prosperous and strive for the education of our children, and may our children live long.

- The boy and girl promise – we complete each other and will be faithful to each other for life.

- The boy and girl promise to be by each other's sides in good and bad times, in prosperity and illness for life.

- The boy says now that you have taken 6 steps with me will you be with me for the rest of my life. To this, the girl replies, "I will always be by your side."

- The boy and girl say now that we are husband and wife, what's mine is yours, and what's yours is mine, and we are together for the rest of our lives for good or bad.

Significance Of the Vows

These vows cover the generally accepted do's and don'ts of a successful marriage.

Janwasa:

This is a place which is organised by the girl's side for the baaratis to stay for the duration of the marriage when the baraat is coming from out of town. Here, the baratis collect (some come directly here) and get rest, change their clothes. Provisions are made for their stay/ snacks and sweets/ tea and coffee. After the baratis have rested, have had something to eat and are ready they leave for the marriage venue.

12. 1ˢᵀ YEAR'S & SUBSEQUENT YEAR'S FESTIVALS

1st Year Festivals

1. Makar Sankranti

A. Gazak and Rewari (to be decided in consultation with the boy's parents).

B. Clothes for the boy/girl/family members (money can be given in lieu).

2. Holi

A. Silver pichkari and bucket

B. Fruits/Sweets

C. Colours (gulal etc)

D. Dry fruits Maala

E. Clothes for the boy and girl (money can be given in lieu)

3. Teej

A. Saree for the girl's mother-in-law

B. Saree or suit for the girl

C. Some jewellery items for the girl

D. Cosmetics and bangles

E. Sweets/Fruits

4. Karva Chauth

A. Saree for the girl's mother-in-law

B. Saree or suit for the girl

C. Baine ka samaan

5. Rakhi

A. Shagun envelope/guinea (depends on individuals)

B. Fruits/Sweets

6. Dusshera

A. Shagun envelope

B. Fruits/Sweets

7. Deepawali

A. Clothes for the boy and girl

B. Silver Hatri for the boy + some silver item

C. Some jewellery items for the girl

D. Dry Fruits approximately 5 kg/Fruits/Sweets

E. Fire crackers

ALL ITEMS, AMOUNTS, ETC., AS PER INDIVIDUAL DESIRES. SIMILAR GIFTS ARE SENT IN EACH SUBSEQUENT YEAR, ALTHOUGH THE AMOUNTS, ETC., MAY BE LESSER.

Subsequent Year's Festivals

1. Makar Sankranti

A. Sweets/fruits/dry fruits

B. Clothes for the boy/girl (money can be given in lieu).

2. Holi

A. Colours (gulaletc)

B. Sweets/Dry fruits

C. Clothes for the boy and girl (money can be given in lieu)

3. Teej

A. Sweets

B. Fruits

C. Clothes for the boy/girl (money can be given in lieu)

4. Karva Chauth

A. Clothes for the boy/girl (money can be given in lieu) Saree or suit for the girl

B. Baine ka samaan

5. Rakhi

A. Mithai

B. Fruits

C. Shagun Envelopes

6. Dusshera

A. Fruits/Sweets/dry fruits

B. Shagun envelope

7. Deepawali

A. Dry Fruits/fruits/sweets

B. Fire crackers

ALL ITEMS, AMOUNTS, ETC., AS PER INDIVIUAL DESIRES.

13. THINGS TO DO FOR & AFTER THE MARRIAGE

Things to Do For & After the marriage

- Locate and finalise the wedding venue

- Finalise the decorator of the marriage venue

- Finalise the menu

- Finalise Photographer

- Finalise the home decoration both inside and outside

- Finalise staying arrangements, food, andconveyance for guests

- Finalise security for the house

- Ladies make-up/Bridal make-up

- Safas for men —especially a kalgi for the boy's safa

- Decoration of the car

- Back Gifts for the in-house guests

- There is a tradition of getting Bhajji boxes made to give to the departing guests. These boxes have sweets/namkeen –

this is to give the people something to eat on the journey back to their homes (had more relevance a few years back)

- Gifts/clothes/money to the domestic and other help who assist to make sure everything goes smoothly

- Panditji Certificate

- Marriage Registration

Documents required for the Registration Certificate:

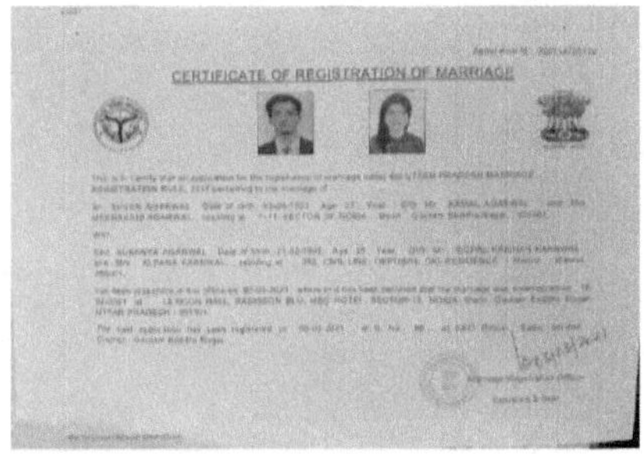

Aadhar Cards of both

PAN Cards of both

High School Marksheets of both

Marriage Photo

Passport size photos 2 each

Panditji Certificate of having performed the marriage

Invitation card